Business Writing: Say More With Less

Master clarity, cut the fluff, and use AI to succeed

Nancy Ancowitz

To Sunshine

Contents

Foreword

"Make this foreword succinct." That's what I kept telling myself after Nancy Ancowitz invited me to compose it.

The goal of business writing is to share information, network, or get someone to take action. It's not to impress them with flowery prose.

People are pressed for time and bombarded daily by emails, texts, and all types of media. Grab their attention. Make your point in as few words as possible while maintaining an appropriate tone.

Professionals rarely read your emails for fun. Why do they care about what you wrote? Your subject lines catch their attention, the first sentence holds their interest, the topic is relevant, and the length looks manageable.

As a career strategist for private clients and an NYU career director and business communication instructor, Nancy has helped thousands of people increase their influence at work, advance their careers, and develop professional brands that stand out from the competition. She specializes in audience-focused business communication. **No wasted words.**

This approach is evident in Nancy's published work, including her groundbreaking book, *Self-Promotion for Introverts®*, and her contributions to *Psychology Today*, *The Times of Israel*, *The New York Times*, and *The Wall Street Journal*.

Business Writing: Say More With Less is not only a guide to laser-sharp business writing; it's an example of it.

Take advantage of this opportunity to refine your writing skills. As a result, you'll make a powerful impact in your professional life.

Ross Brand

5-time #1 International Bestselling Author

Introduction

Dear Current and Emerging Business Leaders,

Care to boost your professional image while saving your readers lots of time? Welcome to the land of short attention spans! Let's entertain this surreal scenario: Your colleagues are riding on a bullet train while emails you've sent them pop up on billboards before their eyes amid lush scenery while emails from their bosses pop up on other billboards.

Think twice if you assume that in the workplace your readers' attention is different. Your job is to capture it in a blink, whether you're emailing, texting, or tweeting. My job is to offer you "do's" and "don'ts" for conveying your thoughts in a flash in writing. You want the professional opportunity, the promotion, or the client? Then, let's buff up your business writing. You'll make every word count, fast-tracking your career. Oh, and how about ChatGPT? Is it the big cheat or the ultimate free assistant? It could be either, so we'll cover that, too—ethics and all.

How to impress your readers:

Your teachers may have taught you to write in long, flowery sentences, in paragraphs that snake as if around a mountain pass, and with fancy words as if each one added a feather to your cap. You want to impress your readers? Then don't whack them in the face with your feathers. Instead, captivate them without frills.

For example, why write "utilize" when "use" conveys the same meaning, yet doesn't sound forced? How about wordy pronouncements of false modesty, like: "in my humble opinion"? No. How about the snooze-inducing: "It seems to me..."? Nooo! Or the self-important: "I'm writing to personally invite you...." Never!

> "Don't use a five-dollar word when a
> fifty-cent word will do."
> - Mark Twain

How to read this guide:

Pick up this guide and put it down anytime. Review the sections that could help you sharpen your proverbial pencil. Check out the resources I share for learning more. Meanwhile, to get the most from this guide, do the writing exercises I've created—with your fingers tapping at your keyboard instead of just noodling them in your head. If you're not feeling energetic, skip to the answer keys in the back of this guide.

What I can help you improve:

Use the list of criteria below to assess your business writing—what you already do well and what you need to improve upon. I will share more about each of these criteria and invite you to actively practice through trial and error.

Business writing criteria list:

1. Clarity

2. Conciseness

3. Crisp subject line and/or headers

4. Grammar, punctuation, and other mechanics (e.g., capitalization; instructions)

5. Active, not passive, language

6. Audience focus; inclusion; appropriate tone

7. Compelling lead sentence and paragraph

8. Well-organized content

9. Clear, logical ending (e.g., call to action, when applicable)

10. ChatGPT—Smart prompts for smart humans

What I cannot help you improve (much):

Grammar, punctuation, and other mechanics of writing are essential to get right, and I recommend seeking out other resources to buff those up. One of my favorites is the classic *The Elements of Style* by William Strunk Jr. and E.B. White.

Another is grammarbook.com, with its rules and quizzes, many of which are free. Supplement them liberally with spellcheckers and grammar checkers. Whether you're navigating English as a second language or you've published academic papers as a native English speaker, take the extra time to double-check your work.

Chapter One

Clarity

Clear writing starts with a clear purpose, making your point as soon as possible in your written communications. Give your readers the context they need from the start.

But how do you do that? Good question. Speaking of questions, make it a habit to ask yourself those rooted in the five Ws—Who, What, When, Where, Why—and the all-important How. This practice, often called the five Ws, will help you anticipate and address your readers' needs effectively. Doing so will provide them with the necessary context without cluttering your message with extraneous information.

Email excerpt—unclear example and clear revision:

Unclear example: Let's meet at Starbucks later this week.

Clear revision: Let's meet just inside the Starbucks at Astor Place on Friday, February 4, at 3 p.m.

Quick explanation:

In the unclear example of an email excerpt above, the Who is implied (you and the email recipient); the What (a meeting); When (later this week) and Where (Starbucks) are vague; the Why is probably understood (or covered in another sentence); and the How is likely irrelevant. Rather than wasting time emailing back and forth to fill in the missing details, why not save time by anticipating and answering questions upfront? In the clear revision, I provide the exact location and date as well as time for the coffee meeting. But I stop short of including unnecessary details like the year or the time zone, since I'm presumably meeting my colleague in a few days and locally. Your turn.

Try it:

Review the following excerpt of an email as if you've received it, and fill in the backstory details as needed (e.g., scenario: your boss asked her nephew to reach out to you for career advice).

Then, ask yourself: What would make the nephew's email excerpt clearer? Which of the Who, What, When, Where, Why, and How questions does the excerpt answer to make the communication clear?

Unclear example from your boss' nephew: As a student, I would like to discuss my career options.

Your clear revision:

____

Exercise: Which of the Who, What, Where,

When, Why, and How questions does it answer that are necessary for conveying a clear message to you, the reader?

Answer key:

Clear revision example: As an HR master's candidate at NYU, I am interested in exploring career options in tech recruiting. Would you be available to provide me advice, at your convenience?

Exercise answer: Who (the student), What (request to discuss career options). Missing: Who (more about the student to provide sufficient context).

Rookie mistakes—DON'T:

- Refer to someone using a pronoun before introducing them by name (or describing them without a name).

- Provide a time without a time zone when you're not sure where your readers are located—or when they're definitely in a different time zone from yours (e.g., 9 a.m., which means many things to many people!).

- Use generic words (e.g., "worked") when specific ones are much clearer (e.g., "organized").

The big idea:

Build in answers to Who, What, When, Where, Why, and How questions your readers need to provide sufficient context and detail. But don't overdo it. Only answer questions that are essential for conveying your message clearly.

Pro tip:

Use jargon (e.g., bizdev, benchmarking) only when you're sure your readers will know what it means. Likewise, spell out the words that acronyms stand for, again, unless you're sure your readers will know them.

Chapter Two

Conciseness

Mark Twain once said, "I didn't have time to write a short letter, so I wrote a long one instead." Don't waste words. Don't bury your most important point in the fifth sentence of the fifth paragraph of your email, business proposal, or professional bio.

I'm on a mission to prompt you to slash unnecessary words. Join me in zapping "wannabe" words, banishing them from your writing. For example, assure me you won't start your cover letters with fatty, dated language like, "To whom it may concern." Inspired by the English playwright Edward Bulwer-Lytton's saying, "The pen is mightier than the sword," go chop-chop to every word-word that your readers don't need-need.

Wordy example and concise revision:

Wordy example: I'm writing to ask you if it would be truly okay for me to take off Tuesday, May 14, 2024, to celebrate my awesome sister's 24th birthday.

Concise revision: May I take a personal day on Tuesday, May 14?

Should you start a cover letter with: "My name is Lee Smith, and I'm writing to apply for the VP of HR position at ACME Corp."? Nooooooo. Why? What can you immediately excise from that? First, your name doesn't belong in the body of a cover letter. That's wasting precious real estate while your readers are blinking! Instead, put it on your letterhead (and in the signature block of your emails). Next, why write that you're writing—as opposed to what? Singing karaoke? Then why waste words on stating the obvious?

Try it:

Review the following excerpts of emails, and build in backstory details, as needed (e.g., who you're writing to and the scenario). Tighten the excerpts while retaining their meaning.

- ***Excerpt 1:*** Would you give me career advice in an effort to aid me in making decisions with respect to my career path in the HR profession?

- ***Excerpt 2:*** Basically, I will send you the report in five weeks' time—definitely before the month of May.

- ***Excerpt 3:*** I am reaching out to you to personally invite you to speak on a panel on machine learning on account of the fact that someone I know said you may be a leader in some of the efforts in that field.

Answer key:

- ***Excerpt example 1**:* Would you give me career advice to help me decide on my HR career path?

- ***Excerpt example 2**:* I will send you the report before May.

- ***Excerpt example 3**:* I'm inviting you to speak on a machine learning panel because of your leadership in the field.

> "The secret of being boring is to say everything."
> -Voltaire

Rookie mistakes—DON'T:

- Use adjectives and adverbs unless you really, absolutely must to convey your phenomenal points; I'm demonstrating this type of bloated writing here in an attempt at levity.

- Use hyperbole and superlatives, unless you intentionally want to exaggerate.

- Repeat words unnecessarily.

The big idea:

Use only the words you need to convey your message, while maintaining an appropriate tone. Feel free to start by writing everything that comes to mind, but then edit it down to your core message. Reminder, writing and editing are two distinct steps.

Pro tip:

Establish your main point at the start—and make everything you write support that point.

Chapter Three

Crisp Subject Line and/or Headers

"A headline should make people stop in their tracks."

-David Ogilvy, founder of Ogilvy & Mather, and often called the "Father of Advertising"

Write email subject lines that save your readers time by getting across your main point in as few words as possible. When you craft your best ones, your recipients often don't even have to open your emails to find out more. Consider using the acronym EOM (End of Message) to convey that you've included all necessary information there and you've left the body of your email blank.

Headers and sub-headers help you get your ideas and requests across to readers quickly, often enabling them to grasp your message just by skimming. This is similar to how the billboards whizzing past your colleagues on that bullet train conveyed their messages instantly. So, when writing your subject lines and headers, be rigorous about cutting all but the most necessary words.

Flabby example and crisp revision:

Flabby subject line example: Announcement: Don't forget to enroll right now in health insurance open enrollment for the year 2025

Crisp revision: Health insurance enrollment deadline—Mon., Apr. 1

Try it:

Read the following sample scenario and subject line.

Sample scenario: You missed your connecting flight while on vacation in Hawaii. Tell your boss that you're delayed in returning to work.

Sample subject line: My delayed return to NYC: Tue., 2/20; Jamie will present recruiting stats

Now, your turn. Follow the other two scenarios and write a clear, concise subject line for each one. If needed, consider adding relevant details.

Scenario: Ask a colleague to write you a recommendation on LinkedIn.

Subject line: ________________________________

Scenario: Offer to help your boss with a dreadfully boring assignment.

Subject line: ________________________________

Answer key:

Scenario 1 example: LinkedIn recommendation request

Scenario 2 example: Offering my help with financial reconciliation project

Rookie mistakes—DON'T:

- Bury the most important part of your subject line to the right, where readers could miss it on their smartphone screens.

- Waste space in your subject lines with your name or other information that you could convey in the body of your emails or signature block.

- Use vague language, leaving your readers unclear about what you need.

- Put a period at the end of a subject line (unless it's an actual sentence).

The big idea:

Writing a succinct subject line or header with few words is harder than a verbose one, since it often takes multiple iterations to distill your message. So, draft and revise it until you make your point quickly, especially considering those who will be reading it from a smartphone.

Pro tip:

Send yourself your draft email with just your subject line and headers to see how much of your message comes across without fleshing out the rest of the text. If necessary, build your email from there.

Chapter Four

Grammar, Punctuation, Other Mechanics

(e.g., capitalization, instructions)

> "In an age of information overload, proper grammar is a lighthouse"
> -Nora Ephron, writer and filmmaker

Just as you wouldn't show up for a job interview in a tattered shirt with spaghetti sauce splotches, why send out a cover letter with grammatical mistakes and typos? You could argue: Employers don't read cover letters, so why waste time writing them? Why should you take a chance by submitting a cover letter that contains even a single typo when other candidates might craft carefully edited ones?

Use all the tools at your disposal—including spellcheckers, grammar checkers, and ChatGPT or other generative AI programs—to wipe your text clean of grammatical errors and typos, the written equivalent of those spaghetti sauce stains. Likewise, many business documents have word-count and character-count requirements, and if you don't follow instructions around them, your text could get cut off.

Grammatical blunder examples and revisions:

Grammatical blunder example #1: My favorite part of my job are the brilliant people I meet.

Grammatically correct example #1: My favorite

part of my job is the brilliant people I meet.

Grammatical blunder example #2: I am eager to join your XYZ team in Google.

Grammatically correct example #2: I am eager to join your XYZ team at Google.

Try it:

Steady this grammatically shaky sentence: I had took the book to the library.

————————————————————————

Answer key:

I took the book to the library.

Rookie mistakes—DON'T:

- Repeat the same mistakes; learn from the errors that spellcheckers and grammar checkers repeatedly find in your writing.

- Start more than two sentences in a row with "I" (or another repeated word).

- Put a period or comma outside closed quotation marks; instead, follow this example of what's correct in US English: Lee said, "Good morning, team."

The big idea:

I'll summarize the importance of grammar, down to the misplaced-comma level by zeroing in on the title of the bestselling book *Eats, Shoots & Leaves*. Consider the meaning of the title now minus the comma: *Eats Shoots & Leaves*. Celebrating that intentionally giddy gaffe, the subtitle says it all: *The Zero Tolerance Approach to Punctuation*.

Regardless of whether you're looking for employment or just want to boost your professional brand, why not make every keystroke contribute to the positive impression you project?

Pro tips:

Create a checklist of your most common mechanical errors—and review your writing against it before circulating it. Why? Most of us make the same errors repeatedly. Determine those errors by using the tools we discussed (e.g., spellcheckers). Here are the top ones I encounter:

- **Verb tenses and subject-verb agreement:** Ensure consistency in verb tenses and agreement in number between subjects and verbs.

- **Prepositions and articles:** Use prepositions (e.g., for, in, at) and articles (a, an, the) correctly to avoid confusion.

- **Singular vs. plural nouns:** Maintain consistency between singular and plural forms to avoid confusion.

- **Punctuation marks:** Apply punctuation marks (e.g., commas, semicolons, colons) properly to convey your meaning clearly.

- **Homophones and spelling consistency:** Don't confuse one homophone with another (e.g., their, there, they're) and maintain consistent spelling.

- **Sentence structure:** Avoid sentence fragments and run-ons; maintain parallel structure in lists.

- **Redundancy and word count:** Eliminate redundant phrases and adhere to word count requirements for clarity and conciseness.

Chapter Five

Active, Not Passive, Language

> "The active voice is usually more direct and vigorous than the passive."
> -William Strunk Jr., *The Elements of Style*

Do you want to punch up sentences that laze around on your lines of text like couch potatoes? Then pry them off their duffs and write in the active voice. Watch those sentences step lively from fluff to concrete by clearly describing who or what is taking an action. So, the subject of your sentence performs the action that the verb describes. Say, what? Let's jog this concept around the block.

Passive language example and active language revision:

Passive example #1: The new initiative was announced.

Active revision #1: Maria announced the new initiative.

Passive example #2: It is often thought that people have a hard time with committing to an exercise routine.

Active revision #2: Many believe that committing to an exercise routine is hard.

Try it:

Now, your turn. Read the sample passive sentences below and turn them into sentences in the active voice. Build in back-story details, as needed.

Passive #1: Approximately 1-4 hours each day are spent procrastinating by an estimated 20% of adults.

Passive #2: **Passive:** An exam is given by the professor twice every semester.

Your turn to make them active:

____

____

Answer key:

Active revision #1: An estimated 20% of adults procrastinate for 1-4 hours each day.

Active revision #2: The professor gives an exam twice every semester.

Rookie mistakes—DON'T:

- Confuse passive language with past tense. Passive language is vague because it doesn't clearly depict who or what is taking an action—and it can be in any tense.

- Use passive language because you've always written that way. To catch it, read your drafts from the last sentence up to the first one. Reviewing your language out of order helps you spot the passive voice.

- Write in the active voice in cases when the passive voice would be more appropriate—when you have good reason not to assign responsibility or blame to a specific party (e.g., when announcing a staff reduction or other bad news).

The big idea:

Passive language is one of the most pernicious clarity and context killers, trumping most other rookie writing errors. Why? It leads your reader into muddy waters—in which they have to work too hard to discern your intention and who is taking action. So, practice writing a couple of active sentences a day until you get this habit down cold. You might even try converting the humorous title of the book *Mistakes Were Made (But Not by Me)* by Carol Tavris, Elliot Aronson, et al. into the active voice. Bonus question: Is the subtitle to that book, *Why We Justify Foolish Beliefs, Bad Decisions, and Hurtful Acts,* in the passive or active voice?

Pro tip:

I joke that it's okay to use passive language—every 50 years. Seriously, find a strong reason to use it, or default to the clearer, more concise active voice.

Chapter Six

Audience Focus, Inclusion, Appropriate Tone

You want your readers' attention? Put yourself in their shoes. Imagine being a Millennial tech manager and receiving a handwritten flyer about trends in rotary phones for your "modern communication needs." Ridiculous, right?

In contrast, mail or email about advances in smartphone technology that saves them time might catch their attention. The more you describe what you have that your readers want or need, the more likely you'll engage them.

Inclusion

An extension of this logic is writing with a lens of inclusion. That means using language that conveys respect for your audience, regardless of their identity or background. This involves avoiding stereotypes and being mindful of cultural differences.

> "I've learned that people will forget what you said, people will forget what you did, but people will never forget how you made them feel."
>
> -Maya Angelou, poet and civil rights activist, and Presidential Medal of Freedom recipient

For example, when emailing colleagues from around the world in December, instead of greeting them with "Merry Christmas," you could write "Happy holidays." Otherwise, some Jewish, Muslim, Hindu, or colleagues of other religions might feel "othered," or marginalized.

Examples of inclusive and non-inclusive language:

Target audience: Software development team (including 10 men and 1 woman)

Non-inclusive example: Hi guys, Welcome aboard! Let's get ready to collaborate productively as a team!

Inclusive revision: Hi team, Welcome aboard! Let's get ready to collaborate productively as a team!

Quick explanation:

The non-inclusive example uses "guys," which excludes women and possibly non-binary individuals. The inclusive revision uses "everyone," making it welcoming to all.

Tone

On a related note, why does tone matter? It sets the stage. Would it be more appropriate to send a slang-filled email with emojis, memes, and dancing GIFs to the hiring manager for your dream job or to your college roommate? Match your tone to your audience. Stop for a moment to consider them before consciously picking an appropriate tone for the occasion (e.g., formal, friendly, upbeat, welcoming, stern). This may sound obvious, but many writers miss this simple step.

Examples of email excerpt with inappropriate and appropriate tone:

Target audience example: HR interns at Pepsi-Co

Example of inappropriate tone: Hey folks, I hope you enjoyed your weekend. We've got some gigunda tasks to tackle. Let's kill 'em before they kill us!

Example of appropriate tone: Good morning awesome HR intern team, I hope you enjoyed your weekend. We look forward to tackling some tough tasks together today.

Quick explanation:

You could argue that the inappropriate tone is too casual and lacks professionalism, which might not be suitable for a workplace setting. The appropriate tone is professional, respectful, and fosters a collaborative environment.

Try it:

Draft a brief email inviting your team to a post-project celebration. Your email should reflect camaraderie and appreciation in one version, and exasperation in another, for comparison.

————————————————————————————————

————————————————————————————————

————————————————————————————————

____

____

____

____

____

Answer key:

Example of camaraderie and appreciation:

Subject: Celebrate our success - Fri., Aug. 5 @ 5 p.m.

Hi Team,

Fantastic work on our budgeting project! Kudos on the collaboration. Let's celebrate this Friday, August 25, at 5 p.m. in Conference Room A with some festive treats and top-notch company.

See you there!

Best,

[Your Name]

Example of exasperation:

Subject: Recovery Time - Post-Budgeting Gathering - Fri., Aug. 5 @ 5 p.m.

Hi Team,

Our budgeting project was brutal this round. We need a break. Let's meet this Friday at 5 p.m. in Conference Room A to decompress and regroup after this whirlwind.

Hope you can make it.

Best,

[Your Name]

Rookie mistakes—DON'T:

- Forget who's on the receiving end and either overshooting with formality or undershooting with casualness.

- Assume all your readers have the same level of technical proficiency, as some may not be familiar with the tools you use.

- Use acronyms and jargon that your audience may not understand.

- Be longwinded; make your points clearly and concisely to save everyone time.

- Ignore cultural differences and sensitivities; instead, respect them to contribute to a safe work environment for everyone.

The big idea:

Use your writing to go beyond conveying information and ideas by viewing your message through the lens of your audience. Doing so can expand your mind and make your messages more impactful to your readers. You'll show that you care about their needs, while also conveying points clearly and concisely.

Pro tip:

Put all your business communications through the "what's in it for my reader" test before hitting "send."

Chapter Seven

Compelling Lead Sentence and Paragraph

> "The most important sentence in any article is the first one. If it doesn't induce the reader to proceed to the second sentence, your article is dead."
> -William Zinsser, author of *On Writing Well*

Snag your readers' attention with a crisp lead sentence and paragraph. How long do you have to get that attention? Set a stopwatch to 5 seconds (about the time it takes to skim up to this point in this paragraph). If you don't get to your point before the beeper goes off, most of your readers will have moved on to the next email, text, or other input vying for their attention. Caveat: You may get a few more seconds if you're their boss, big client, or other pivotal player in their professional life. So, treat your lead sentence and paragraph as a movie trailer. If you don't capture your readers' attention with the snippet, why would they bother with the movie?

Example of a weak lead sentence and revision:

Example of a weak lead: I am writing to inform you about our very latest HR policy that might interest some of you or your colleagues.

Revised lead sentence: Our summer hours are here: You're welcome to leave the office at 3 p.m. every Friday through August 30.

Quick explanation:

The original lead sentence is wordy and vague. The revised version captures the readers' attention, immediately providing them with useful specifics.

Try it:

Write the lead sentence for an email, executive summary, or other business document using the sample scenario below as a guide. Summarize your key point in your lead sentence and add supporting details that your readers need to know. Then, write the rest of the paragraph, providing your other points and logic to support them, if necessary.

Sample scenario: Request a meeting to plan the onboarding of your organization's summer interns. Fill in backstory details (e.g., department names, type of summer internship, dates/times) as needed.

____

____

____

____

Answer key (one of many possible compelling lead sentences):

Let's meet on Wednesday, August 21, at 10 a.m. to finalize our summer intern onboarding plans.

Rookie mistakes—DON'T:

- Start with unnecessary information, like your name, which belongs in the signature block of an email.

- Bury the lead (also spelled lede) by beginning with less important information.

- Write a wordy opening sentence or paragraph (e.g., fluffed up with unnecessary adjectives and adverbs).

The big idea:

Get to the point from the start. You'll save your readers time while conveying a professional image as a clear, precise communicator.

Pro tip:

Read your writing out loud—or better yet, use a screen reader. By hearing a machine-generated voice read it, you'll further test how engaging your message is.

Chapter Eight

Well-Organized Content

> "Good prose is like a windowpane. The clearer the structure, the more the content shines through."
>
> -George Orwell, Author of 1984 and Animal Farm

Imagine you're a hiring manager reviewing 100 cover letters and resumes for a position. Halfway through the pile, you reach Cameron's cover letter. For three paragraphs, Cameron rambles about why he's the "perfect candidate," citing irrelevant skills, experience, and career goals that don't align with the position.

Meanwhile, a former boss of Cameron's—a friend of the hiring manager—recommended him for the role, but Cameron doesn't mention this until the fourth paragraph. Organizing your thoughts before writing them, whether for a cover letter, resume, professional bio, or other business communications, saves your readers time, especially when they're skimming. Oh, and never be audacious enough to call yourself "a perfect candidate."

Example of a disorganized text message and revision:

Example of a disorganized text message (out of the blue): Hi Jordan, Do you want to meet later or Friday? I wanted to tell you that we have several issues with the project. Let's get the resources he mentioned.

Revised, well-organized text message: Hi Jordan, We have three pressing challenges on the XYZ project. Let's take Leo up on his team's offer to help. Can we meet via Zoom today at 2 p.m. ET or this Friday at 9 a.m. ET?

Quick explanation:

The first text is wordy (e.g., "I wanted to tell you that…") and chaotic. It lacks context, especially since the recipient may be in the middle of another priority. The message raises more questions than it answers: What project is the sender referring to? Who is offering resources? When is the sender available to meet? The revision immediately states the problem and proposes a solution. It offers specific times for a meeting and makes the problem, proposed solution, and call to action clear.

Try it:

Craft a text asking a colleague for help with a project to meet a crucial 5 p.m. deadline today. Include backstory details (e.g., specify the project and the type of help you need) to make your message clear.

Answer key (one of many possible well-organized texts):

Hi Alex, We need help with our cost-reduction project to meet today's 5 p.m. deadline. Would you assist with the final quality checks?"

Rookie mistakes—DON'T:

- Scatter your points across your message.

- Write in vague terms that may confuse your recipients.

- Bury your most important point.

- Include multiple unrelated topics in a single communication.

The big idea:

The text message example shows that you can convey well-organized points in a few succinct sentences. With emails, use the subject line to highlight your key point before the recipient even opens your note. Use headers, sub-headers, and bullets to help organize your points, making your message easier to read at a glance.

Pro tip:

Craft an outline to organize your thoughts, prioritizing the most important points before writing your drafts.

Follow the guidance in this chapter to improve clarity, reduce redundancy, and tighten the writing for more impactful communication.

Chapter Nine

Clear, Logical Ending

> "Begin with the end in mind."
> -Stephen Covey, Author of *The 7 Habits of Highly Effective People*

Why do you need a crisp ending to your written communications? I'll answer a question with a question: Is your message succinct and audience-focused from start to end? If so, you may not need to add anything else.

However, when wrapping up a detailed email, report, proposal, or even a slide deck, you may want to end with a recap, action items, or next steps. To determine whether you need an ending, per se, ask yourself whether you've conveyed your point clearly and concisely while using language that will resonate with your readers. If so, you're finished. If not, then determine what's missing.

Example of a vague ending and clear revision:

Example of a vague ending: Let me know if this is good as is.

Revised ending, with a clear call to action: Please confirm by Friday, August 9, at 5 p.m., if you approve sending this proposal to the XYZ client.

Quick explanation:
The original ending is vague and lacks a clear request. The revised version is direct and specific, providing a clear action item and deadline.

Try it:

Craft an ending for an email confirming a client meeting.

____

____

____

____

Answer key (one of many possible correct endings):

Please confirm our meeting on Thursday, January 5, at 2 p.m. at your Midtown office. Looking forward to finalizing our plans.

Rookie mistakes—DON'T:

- **Be vague:** Ambiguity leads to confusion. Instead of saying, "Let me know if this is good as is," specify what you mean by "this" and include when you'd like the reader to reply. Clarity around the subject and timeline prevents misunderstandings.

- **Waste time:** Failing to include next steps or action items may require unnecessary follow-up, wasting both your time and your reader's. Whenever applicable, conclude with clear instructions or expectations to streamline communication.

- **Overwhelm with new information:** Introducing new topics at the end can detract from your main message and overwhelm your readers. Instead, wrap up clearly and crisply.

The big idea:

Whether you conclude by underscoring your key point in a tweet or summarize next steps with deadlines and accountability for your team in an email, your ending matters. It is a chance to reinforce your message and drive action. Be purposeful about how you wrap up your written communications. This approach ensures that you position yourself as a clear, intentional communicator who doesn't waste time dilly-dallying!

Pro tip:

Make sure you clearly identify yourself, including your full name, nickname (if applicable), and contact information in a signature block in your emails. Here is an example:

Riley Carter

HR Business Partner at XYZ Company

linkedin.com/in/firstnamelastname

firstnamelastname@email.com

555-555-5555

Chapter Ten

ChatGPT, et al.

> "AI is one of the most profound things we're working on as humanity. It's more profound than fire or electricity, but we must harness it responsibly."
>
> -Sundar Pichai, CEO of Alphabet and Google

Can you actually write like a pro and ace your career without using your brain? Well, sort of. Not really. Maybe. But definitely not ethically.

Confused? Let me break it down. I primarily use one of the most popular generative AI programs, ChatGPT, and for simplicity, it will be my main point of reference in this discussion.

Getting started with ChatGPT

Generative AI programs like ChatGPT (developed by OpenAI) are advanced tools that create human-like text based on the prompts you provide. They can draft emails, write essays, answer questions, and engage in written conversation.

ChatGPT is among the most popular, along with other tools like Google's Gemini, Claude by Anthropic, and Jasper by Jasper AI, each serving different text creation needs. ChatGPT generated this text based on the following prompt I gave it: "Please give me a 1-2 sentence description of generative AI programs like ChatGPT for those who are new to it. You can lead with mentioning ChatGPT, but also mention that there are other popular generative AI programs - and three other top ones."

I'm a fan of using ChatGPT as my always-on digital assistant. I interact with it much like I would with a human, enjoying many of the perks without the quirks. No need to swap tips on killer pickleball spin serves, fuel the water-cooler gossip mill, or coordinate complicated coffee runs—ChatGPT cuts to the chase.

As you may have noticed in my example in the inset box, I even type "please" when giving prompts, as if I'm writing to a colleague—it's just that natural!

ChatGPT is my go-to tool for beating the blank page—it often jumpstarts my writing process. I type in a few prompts (AI jargon for the text or question you input), and in seconds, it spits out drafts faster than you can say "writer's block."

That's usually all I need to get started. It's also a powerful tool for catching and correcting mechanical errors in my writing—grammar, spelling, punctuation—so my inner perfectionist can rest easy.

Ethical use and transparency

Now, let's shift the focus to you: Here's how you can use ChatGPT effectively and ethically. While ChatGPT's capabilities are vast, the focus here is on how it can assist with your business writing—ethically. Use generative AI as more of a collaborator than a ghostwriter. It's a low-cost or free assistant that works on your terms, ready whenever you are.

But as the superhero Spider-Man reminds us, "With great power comes great responsibility," echoing the thoughts of 18th-century French philosopher Voltaire. Your responsibility? Credit your human sources and be transparent about using generative AI.

Let's be clear: Using AI doesn't mean outsourcing your thinking. You're still responsible for ensuring that your content is accurate, ethical, and aligned with your voice. That's where transparency comes in.

Be open about your use of AI, even if it's just as a drafting tool. Transparency builds trust and shows that while you embrace technology, you're committed to integrity. While it might be acceptable to use ChatGPT for drafting a cover letter or LinkedIn bio, it's essential to disclose its use when readers expect your original work, such as in academic papers.

Tools like Turnitin, GPTZero, and Originality.ai are designed to detect AI-generated content. If they catch you hiding it in these contexts, you can damage your credibility. So, be upfront from the start—and remember, even with disclosure, you shouldn't rely on AI for your entire document.

Your voice

Just as my voice is distinct, so is yours—despite ChatGPT's impressive talent for mimicry across millions of topics and in over 50 languages. Sure, it can draft your next tweet as if Shakespeare, Maya Angelou, or Confucius had written it, but it can't replicate the footprints that map your journey, the fingerprints that identify you, or the imprints you leave on the world. That's what gives your voice its true power and authenticity.

Accuracy and smart use of generative AI

Generative AI is error-prone. I once asked ChatGPT to find studies on a specific topic in peer-reviewed, double-blind research. It produced articles from top journals with titles that sounded spot-on.

But upon closer inspection, four out of the five articles were completely fabricated. This taught me an important lesson: Always verify the information ChatGPT provides. It's your responsibility to ensure accuracy. The quality of the output depends on the clarity and precision of your input. The saying, "garbage in, garbage out," applies here.

While that phrase has become somewhat of a cliché, it underscores an important point: The quality of ChatGPT's output hinges, at least partly, on how well you craft your prompts.

Be specific, zero in on the information your audience needs, and provide clear context. The more refined your prompts, the better the AI's output.

Examples of responsible and irresponsible AI use:

Responsible use of AI: I used AI tools to help draft our marketing plan, outlining our initial strategy. After careful review and refinement, I am confident it aligns with our goals. Please review the plan and share your thoughts by Tues., Oct. 1.

Irresponsible use of AI: I drafted our marketing plan. Please review it and share your thoughts by Tues., Oct. 1.

This approach over-relies on AI, suggesting a lack of personal input or critical review, which can undermine credibility.

Try it:

Draft the body of an email using ChatGPT to summarize a meeting and propose next steps. Build in backstory details. Ensure clarity and transparency about AI usage.

____

____

____

____

Answer key (one of many ways to disclose your use of AI):

Following our meeting this morning, I drafted a summary and outlined next steps, with an as-sist from ChatGPT. Please review the attached document and share your feedback by Thurs., Jan. 15.

Rookie mistakes—DON'T:

- **Rely solely on AI for sensitive communication:** AI can generate content quickly, but it may lack the empathy and understanding required for delicate situations.

- **Ignore the need for thorough review:** AI can make mistakes, and it's crucial to review all generated content for accuracy and appropriateness before sending it out.

- **Hide your use of AI in professional contexts where transparency is expected:** While it may be fine to use AI for drafting a cover letter or social media post, be transparent about its use in academic, publishing, or formal business settings.

- **Over-rely on AI-generated jargon:** AI often generates phrases that sound technical but may not resonate with your audience. Simplify and personalize the content to ensure clarity.

The big idea:

AI tools like ChatGPT are powerful aids in business writing, but they are just that—tools. Use them to enhance your productivity and creativity, but always maintain control over the final output. Ethical, transparent, and thoughtful use of AI in writing will strengthen your professional communication and build trust with your audience.

Pro tip:

When using ChatGPT or any other generative AI tool, remember that the quality of your output directly reflects the clarity of your input. Craft specific, thoughtful prompts and always review the AI's suggestions critically. Be on the lookout for inaccuracies, bias, or overly complex language, and double-check facts through trusted sources. While these tools can enhance your productivity, your voice and judgment are irreplaceable—so keep the final say in your hands.

Conclusion

This guide equips you with practical strategies for clear, concise, and professional writing that resonates with your audience. Use the 10 criteria as a checklist for crafting lead sentences, organizing your content effectively, and eliminating grammar mistakes.

Additionally, we've discussed how to ethically integrate AI tools like ChatGPT into your writing process while ensuring your distinct voice remains intact.

Remember, strong communication is a major asset in your career. Before hitting "send," review your message thoroughly. Even if you polish it along the way, make sure to do a final check. Here are a few approaches I've already mentioned, plus some new ones to add to your editorial toolkit:

- Read your writing out loud

- Ask someone to read it to you

- Review it from the last sentence to the first, sharpening your focus on details

- Print it out (when the stakes are high)

- Listen to it on a text-to-speech app (e.g., Speechify)

- Use a spellchecker and grammar checker (e.g., Grammarly)

- Paste your language into ChatGPT to check logic, tone, flow, as well as grammar and spelling

I usually use a combination of several of these. It's worth repeating that AI tools, spellcheckers, and grammar checkers make mistakes (i.e., all. the. time!). They will identify potential errors, but you are the final judge and guardian of your professional brand.

Appendix A

Professional bio examples

Crafting a bio for LinkedIn—or any professional platform—not only creates a strong narrative for your brand but also provides a foundation for your cover letters. Whether you write it in the first or third person is up to you. Your bio also works as a starting point for your elevator pitch or self-introduction, in person or online.

Just as you tailor cover letters, adjust your pitch to suit the audience—whether in an interview or a chat with a speaker at a conference. Remember: your delivery should never sound scripted and should invite conversation.

LinkedIn headline and bio 1:

Tingting Zhou's headline: Global Compensation Expert | M.S. in HR from NYU

Tingting's bio: Tingting is an HR compensation expert with McKinsey & Company experience who develops scalable, sustainable, and equitable programs that attract and retain top talent. She specializes in global benchmarking and market analysis, and designs compensation structures (base pay, variable pay, and long-term incentive plans) that align with business strategy.

Tingting has managed projects for a >$1B tech unicorn CEO, eliminating pain points and exceeding time, budget, and functionality goals. She builds automated dashboards for C-suite executives to make well-informed decisions quickly. She also creates streamlined tools that empower cross-functional stakeholders with decision-making autonomy in sync with an organization's mission.

Tingting earned an M.S. in Human Resources from NYU. She has lived in four countries and is trilingual: fluent in English and Korean, and a native Chinese speaker. Tingting is a licensed scuba diver who enjoys exploring the depths—from sea to shining sea.

KEY QUALIFICATIONS

• Global Benchmarking & Market Pricing & Market Analysis
• Compensation Structure Design / Broad-Based Compensation
• Base Pay
• Variable Pay / Short-term Incentives / Bonus Model
• Long-term Incentive Plan
• Job Architecture
• Project Management
• HRIS & People System / Process & Data Flow
• Workday / BambooHR / PeopleSoft
• Automation & Tooling
• HR Dashboards / Data Analysis & Visualization
• Cost Management

- Advanced Excel & Google Sheets
- Financial Literacy
- Human Capital Management
- English / Chinese / Korean

Industries: Professional Services, Fin-tech, Travel, Ad-Tech, Public Utilities, Manufacturing, Management Consulting, Non-profit, Aerospace, Auto, Retailing, Single Family Office

Tingting Zhou's LinkedIn headline, "Global Compensation Expert | M.S. in HR from NYU," captures her qualifications beyond her current job title. This approach showcases her broader professional brand and the value she brings to the field.

Her headline is a strategic way to highlight her expertise, which is valuable whether she's looking to build her network, explore new opportunities, or simply establish her presence in the industry.

LinkedIn headline and bio 2:

Dhanush Raj's headline: M.S. in Mathematics in Finance at NYU Courant | Emerging Quantitative Researcher

Dhanush's bio: I am an M.S. in Mathematics in Finance candidate at NYU Courant with a first-class honors B.Sc. in Data Science. With an extensive background in data-driven research, I excel in developing and validating mathematical models. I am eager to apply my comprehensive analytical and interpersonal skills to a quantitative research team and collaborate on machine learning projects in finance.

Research & Analytical Skills

- 10+ years' Python experience; strong foundation in statistics, probability, machine learning

- Highest honors thesis on tractable optimization, showcasing expertise in mathematical modeling

- Innovation in options pricing through deep learning, gradient boosting, and robust optimization

- Co-authorship of a data-driven research paper published by IEEE

Communication & Teamwork Skills

- Expertise in presenting and publishing complex findings to diverse audiences

- Leadership of university's sports team from year-long losing streak to regional silver medal

- Club size increase of 300% through extensive targeted outreach

- Highly collaborative with strong competitive spirit

Appendix B

Cover letter example

By adapting the core elements of your bio, you can efficiently tailor your cover letters to specific opportunities while maintaining consistency in how you present yourself across different platforms.

Example:

Dhanush Raj 777-777-7777 // firstnamelastname@nyu.edu // linkedin.com/in/dhanush25raj

September 4, 2025

Hiring Professional

XXXXXXXXXX

New York, NY

Re: Quantitative Research Position (#12345)

Dear Firstname Lastname [or Dear Hiring Professional],

I recently had the pleasure of meeting with [Firstname Lastname], who shared her positive experiences as a quantitative analyst at [XXXXX]. I am a candidate for an M.S. in Mathematics in Finance at NYU Courant with a first-class honors B.Sc. in Data Science. With an extensive background in data-driven research, I excel in developing and validating mathematical models, and I am enthusiastic about joining [XXXXX] at [YYYYY].

Highlights of my qualifications include:

Research & Analytical Skills

- 10+ years' Python experience; strong foundation in statistics, probability, and machine learning

- Highest honors thesis on tractable optimization, showcasing expertise in mathematical modeling

- Innovation in options pricing through deep learning, gradient boosting, and robust optimization

- Co-authorship of a data-driven research paper published by IEEE

Communication & Teamwork Skills

- Expertise in presenting and publishing complex findings to diverse audiences

- Leadership of university's sports team from a yearlong losing streak to a regional silver medal

- Club size increase of 300% through extensive targeted outreach

- Highly collaborative with a strong competitive spirit

I am eager to leverage my data-driven research experience, robust academic knowledge, and strong interpersonal skills to benefit [XXXXX] at [YYYYY], which I admire for its collaborative culture, commitment to technology, and abundant learning opportunities.

Sincerely,
Dhanush

Appendix C

Thank-you note example

The thank-you note below is effective because it features a clear, concise subject line that conveys the purpose of its message.

It is audience-focused, tailoring the content to the recipient's input and expertise, and it expresses gratitude with crisp, specific details.

The sender also distinguishes herself by highlighting her professional focus and offering a relevant article to pique the recipient's interest. This thoughtful touch reinforces their connection and adds value to the exchange.

Example (after a coffee chat):

To: Jo Jones

From: Sandy Davis

Date: January 2, 2025

Subject: Thank you - nailing my elevator pitch

Hi Jo,

Thank you for our coffee chat yesterday! I am grateful for your feedback about my elevator pitch. Instead of simply critiquing it, you asked the right questions, encouraging me to think more analytically. I appreciated your suggestions about conveying my passion for recruiting more clearly and concisely. I also liked your advice about describing my transferable skills.

My valuable takeaways from our meeting include: making my most important points first, targeting my audience using keywords, and quantifying my accomplishments.

If you are ever interested in the latest trends in recruiting, please consider me a resource. Meanwhile, I thought you'd be interested in this article on [XXXX]: [LINK]

Thank you again for generously sharing your expertise.

Kind regards,
Sandy

Sandy Davis

Master's Candidate in HR at NYU | Emerging Recruiter

https://www.linkedin.com/in/firstnamelast-name123

firstnamelastname@nyu.edu

888-888-8888

Appendix D

ChatGPT: Empowering Introverts in the World of Writing

Here's to noodling quietly with the collective zeitgeist!

One of my greatest sources of joy since late November 2022 has been collaborating with ChatGPT—together with my graduate business students and coaching clients—to help them land professional opportunities. How? By enhancing their writing. Also, I've delighted in moderating discussions about chatbots for a variety of professional and academic organizations, engaging in multiple panelists' perspectives.

Some insist the chatbot flashfire setting the world ablaze is subsuming our ability to think critically. They protest that this conflagration is obliterating jobs, blurring the bounds of originality, and snuffing out creativity. Some express a fear of being replaced by bots, snuffing out their livelihood and career prospects.

Flickering from the firepits of the zeitgeist, questions shoot up: Are we now useless at telling the difference between what's human versus computer generated? Is ChatGPT a multi-purpose tool like flint that you can use for good or evil? Should you be ashamed if you still haven't even touched that tool (that some call a weapon)?

Yo, Prometheus, titan god of fire, how can I just sit by with my grad students and clients, giddily toasting marshmallows beside the blaze? As an introvert, I'm lit up by this tool that some say threatens the destruction of humanity—yet I see its potential for creation.

Artificial intelligence versus my native intelligence sparks my own shame that I'll never know enough about what I'm talking about as my internal gag order demands my silence until I can achieve the impossible. Counterbalancing that, I purse my lips into a rumble of raspberries that fan the flames and sometimes just bask in their toastiness. Echoing that, my panels of experts insist there are no experts, since we're all figuring this out. Yes, together(ish).

Still, I am quasi-secretly intrigued by ChatGPT as a sparring partner. It doesn't judge me. It apologizes when it doesn't really "get" my prompts or queries, with its expansive mega-brain that mops up all the bits of thoughts, news, and fake news out there, and spits them out, never holding back.

So, here's more of what I like about "collaborating" with chatbots:

1. **Blank page terminator.** Chatbots like ChatGPT can get you unstuck and give

you a jump-start. Are they more of a chemical fire starter than a thinking partner? Without them, I rub two sticks together with rarely a flicker. So, even when ChatGPT generates bland ideas, it spurs my critical, competitive mind to say: "I can do better." My clients embrace it similarly.

2. **Idea generator.** Writing specific, clear prompts, and then asking the chatbot to pump out a bunch of ideas, can help you by creating a smorgasbord of options. Then you pick and choose. Or tell it that you want more of this and less of that. Make it more quantitative. Pithier. Targeted at anthropologists or bankers or clowns. Whatever. The other day, it helped a client of mine, who does something that sounds dull in the financial world, spicing it up with 10 different metaphors. He picked his favorite three and we massaged the text into some-

thing that spoke to him so he can speak to the CEOs who can hire him.

3. **Grammarian.** This is one of the more obvious applications. I'm gobsmacked at the speed at which ChatGPT, even the free version I still use, picks out grammatical errors, listing and fixing them. Again, giving it smart prompts helps. So, rather than typing "correct all my mistakes," I prefer to tell the bot exactly what I want it to do. I like to see what it considers errors, and then I get to adjudicate, seeing if I agree. How? Er, sometimes just Googling whether the proverbial "affect" is really an "effect."

I love interacting with computers—at least some of the time. Same with people. Here's what still rankles me:

1. **Not trustworthy.** It's well known that you can't fully trust the information that chatbots spit out. Collaborate smartly

with chatbots by questioning and double-checking anything they provide you. Remember that they're only as smart as the bazillion bits of data they're aggregating.

2. **Unstable, overloaded systems.** I noticed that especially in the early days when ChatGPT came out, about half the time I logged in, the system was overloaded. So when I presented it to my NYU graduate students, it wasn't working.

3. **Flaky at following instructions (e.g., "eliminate redundancy").** Sometimes, ChatGPT half listens. But that's just like most people.

So, ChatGPT: friend or foe? That was the name of one of the virtual panel events I facilitated recently. A few months beforehand, the host noticed that many other events happened to have the same title. We resolved not to ask a chatbot for a better name. No pride in that—we just used our brains (or not!).

Originally published on July 13, 2023, on Nancy Ancowitz's Psychology Today *blog.*

Appendix E

How Introverts Gain Visibility by Tackling Writer's Block

A Personal Perspective: Here's to sending your inner critic for coffee.

More than a year ago, I collaborated with an impossibly gifted writer/actor/video expert named Michael Kinney on a video in which he played my inner critic, Ludley. This is an open letter to Michael since I dropped the ball on our working relationship. The video was to accompany a proposal for a second book I struggled to write.

Dear Michael,

I'm ashamed of how long it's taken me to follow up. I loved, loved collaborating on a teaser video for the book proposal I was wrestling with for Top Ways Not to Bore Your Virtual Audiences Silly: How to Dazzle on Zoom (et al.).

Remember the literary agent Maude [a nickname as are all names in this post]? She was psyched about my book idea and said she could "sell" it to publishers once I sent her a formal proposal. After a year, I finally completed that proposal, which included several chapters of the book plus our five-minute teaser video.

She was so excited that now she's up and retired.

Why did I take so long? Writer's block.

Writing has always been my biggest challenge – harder even than self-promotion for this introvert. Also, I got distracted by personal emergencies. One included my father dying. He left me feeling I should reach for the stars: If I couldn't win the Nobel/Pulitzer-You-Name-It Prize, I shouldn't bother. It's easy to blame parents. However, it feels more alive to defy their projections.

I dusted off the names of three other agents who approached me – a dozen years ago when they pursued me.

But now? "Nancy, who?"

I ran the names of the three agents by my agent – if I can still call Maude that. I told her I pissed off the Plan B one, Ludmilla, when I turned her down for the less fancy Maude. Maude said she's known Ludmilla for decades and that she always sounds pissed, but she's just passionate. We checked Ludmilla's Fancy Literary Agency website: She's no longer taking on new books.

Plan C: Simon, who approached me 15 years ago. From a Google search, he's still in business. His website states a "don't call us, we'll call you" policy and that authors can submit "cold" but should never, ever, follow up.

Agents are like that. After Maude said Simon looked impressive, I submitted my proposal to him.

Weeks went by. Nada.

Now we're at Plan D, Rory, who reached out to me back when. I pinged him on LinkedIn. Ten weeks later, nada. I've been ghosted by more important people.

Harder to admit: Maude sent my proposal to agents in her circle before I groveled my way down the Old Agent Reachout path.

One wrote they were trying to sell a similar book idea – without success.

Another wrote that the idea sounds more like a magazine article.

Yet another wrote that the time to have come out with this book was the start of COVID-19.

Back to you, Michael. I buoyantly created that

video with you promoting a book that may never happen.

I still loathe social media, so I'll never be an influencer. I'm not even on Instagram. Should I aspire more to TikTok? So, I don't know about this introvert selling a book on her own. Or paying the equivalent of college tuition to have someone pretend to be me and sell it for me.

Of course, first, I need to write the balance of the book. Maybe I should autogenerate it with the AI chatbot phenomenon chatGPT. While my head is in the cyberclouds, maybe I can find an avatar to sell the book for me. Yo, AgentGPT!

I'm still not up for self-publishing. Why? Ludley is a snob. Yes, I know a zillion authors and can ask for introductions to their agents. I introduced many to Maude over the years. But she never "bit." The Fussbudget Agent Theory is confirmed. They're always looking for something else. I got lucky to have Maude, Ludmilla, Simon, and Rory knocking at my door ages ago.

I miss you playing my inner critic with humor – and regret having replaced you with the real McCoy over the past year while my fingers froze on my keyboard. While waiting for Maude to retire.

I'm going out on a limb, sharing a glimpse at this teenage diary rant-whine. I feel exposed, yet this is a stretch that is worth making.

I'm taking a risk to be vulnerable, even as a quiet introvert – in case others can relate, offering this letter to possibly touch a heart, a mind.

I miss you as my inner critic. What do you say?

With gratitude,

Nancy

PS to self:

Ludley, go for coffee for a few minutes (so I can't hear you trying to drown me out).

Here's what I know Michael relates to: When I'm asked how long it took me to write Self-Promotion for Introverts, I jokingly reply 40 years. But it's no joke. I'm wailing inside. Then there's the self-promotion piece. I know I wrote a book on that – especially for introverts. Like me, Michael, and half the population. So, I have all the answers? No. I'm not suggesting "do as I say." Instead, like many things, self-promotion, especially for introverts, is a work in progress, not "one and done."

It takes feeding the beast – or, better, remembering your gifts, and getting out and offering them. Fine, from the comfort of your keyboard or Zoom. Don't let fear be the reason you're not getting where you want to go and serving those who need your gifts.

Here's my checklist to get back on track when Ludley fusses at me:

1. Inhale, exhale.

2. Feel my feet on the ground.

3. Focus on something other than my in-

ner chatter and replace negative messages with something productive, claim-
ing that mind real estate for something
more alive – that blossoms and bears
fruit.

Let's share in that bounty.

Oh, hi, Ludley. Thanks for the coffee. Could you
go back and add some sugar to that?

*Originally published on January 14, 2023, on Nan-
cy Ancowitz's* Psychology Today *blog.*

A Quick Favor...

Now that you've finished this book, I'd love to hear your thoughts. What resonated with you the most? Was there anything that you wish were different?

I value your feedback and would appreciate if you would take a moment to leave a review on Amazon. I read every review and use your input to make my future books even better.

I am grateful for your support!
Nancy Ancowitz

Leave a review:

nancyancowitz.com/book/business-writing

Gratitude

Business writing books can be boring. Wouldn't you rather read the ingredients on a cereal box or an app's terms of service? In that spirit, I wrote this guide to help you advance in your career by writing clear, concise, audience-focused language. I can't wait to share it with my graduate students at NYU. I'm also making it available to a wider audience, thanks to the countless clients and workshop participants who have entrusted me with the often-vulnerable process of polishing their presence on "paper" and in front of an audience.

Because I wanted to complete the book before the next semester started, I knew that going the traditional agent-and-publisher route, which typically takes 12-24 months, was not an option. Shortly before the fall semester, I asked Ross Brand, a best-selling author, for his thoughts. He offered to transform my manuscript into a book within a few weeks. He provided me with outstanding guidance, going above and beyond on everything from the book layout to the cover design to the keywords that help readers find the book. Ross, thank you for opening my eyes to the world of indie publishing.

A whopping thank you also to Pam Kanner, a "word gymnast," for helping me catapult this book out the door while standing on her head.

I am grateful to Monica Glina, Ed.D., for thoughtfully reviewing an early draft of this guide. You lent your deep expertise in pedagogy, educational technology, and learner engagement to enrich what I wrote.

A special acknowledgment goes to my NYU colleague Jack Appleman and his book, *10 Steps to Successful Business Writing*. For more than a decade, I've used your book as a go-to guide for my graduate students and continue to recommend it.

Thanks to Mike Barlow, who describes himself as the most prolific author you've never heard of. With more than 40 books under your belt, you have inspired me to pursue this project and see it through to completion. As a business communication professor as well as an esteemed mentor to many of my grad students, you have provided valuable insights in our ongoing dialogue about excellent writing in a world of ChatGPT.

Thank you to my fellow writers, mentors, mentees, and other muses, including Nil Demircubuk, Lisa Provost, Kathryn Britton, Suze Allen, and my private clients.

Shout-outs to other colleagues, friends, and family members whom I deeply value: Carol Abrams, Karen Abrams Gerber, Ed.D., Elaine

Ahlberg, Drew Alexander, Richard & Ellen, Allie, Jon, and Valerie Ancowitz, Rebecca Arora, Daniel Baitch, Keisha Berkley, Kathy Caprino, Carolina Ceniza-Levine, Bryan Chandler, Ellis Chase, Allison Cheston, Glenn Chiarello, DDS, Dorie Clark, Aren Cohen, Michael Cole, Liz Colodny, MBA, David E. Cooley, Michael Crockett, Stephanie Cziczo, MSc, MPA, Lynne Davidson, Ph.D., Dewey Davis-Thompson, Jeanne Drevas, Sid Efromovich, Morgan Ertel, Vanessa Esparza, Jen Figtreefarm, Mary Fields, Christine Fischer, Anne Fizzard, Nancy Friedberg, Dina Friedel, Fernanda Garcia, Shakti Gattegno, Donatella Giacometti, Hope King-Gilbert, Samuel Goldring, DPM, Julie Winkle Guilioni, Jiani Guo, Bonnie Halpern, Rosie Hancock, Kerry Hannon, Stephanie Mieras Hansen, SPHR, SHRM-SCP, Tas Hasan, Alex Jack, Carrie Jaquith, Jennifer Kahnweiler, Ph.D., MJ & Barry, Joe, and Benny Kanner, Dana Kaplan, Roger Kastner, Debra Keenan, Koko Keller, Janet Kenney, Ha Kyung Kim, Carl Kissin, Mahesh Krisnamurti, Brian Krzewinski, Greg Lieberman, Ph.D., Marianna Lead, Soo Lee, Mika Liss, Adam Ma, Paul Marrandino, Senia Maymin, Julie Miller, Bonnie Mincu, Lourdes Olvera-Marshall, Heidi Rome, Steve Orr, Basi Perkins, Andrey Pimenov, Susan Plawsky, Sarah Pletts, Tomer Porian, Nol Putnam, Elliott Rabin, Jenilee Ramos, Marjorie Ramos, Barbara Rubin, Paul Rátz de Tagyos, Lynne Robyn, Morgan Callan Rogers, Janet Rosen, Janet Rossbach, Moshmi Sanagavarapu, Carol Schaechter, Ilene Schaffer, MAPP, MA, PCC, Gerry Seidman, Moira Shaughnessy, Devan Sipher, Amit Srivastav, Jan Stanley, Carol Stark, Lisa Stathoplos, Leigh Strimbeck, Vincent Suppa, Roland Tec, Kelvin Tsang, MS, CPA, CAMS, CISA, Sophia Glezos Voit, Jennifer (Auer) Voldins, CFA, Emily Westerman, Sarah Wheat, Glen Wolyner, Nicole Woodard, Michele Wucker, Tony Yang, Tingting Zhou, Shoya Zichy.

Thank you to my colleagues at the NYU Division in Programs in Business for upholding the reputation of our HR Master's program: Negar Farakish, PMP, Ed.D., Anna Tavis, Ph.D., Mike

Valentine, J.D., Ph.D., Heather Askildsen, Chantal Gomes, Lisa Hoang.

Big thanks to my colleagues, alums, and mentors to my students at the NYU Courant Institute of Mathematical Sciences. You inspire my students to put their best foot forward in words—written and spoken: Petter Kolm, Shizhu Liu, Katie Lynn, M.Ed.,Ariane Saney, Ian Adelson, Charles Carre, Juma Charyyev, CN Chen, Annemarie DiGiacomo Morris, ACC, CPC, PHR, SHRM-CP, MS, ELI-MP, Clare Finnegan, Scott Gruder, Jingsheng (David) Huang, Oksana Kitaychik, Ashish Kohli, Christos Koutsoyannis, Edison Lee, Iris Li, Jiaxuan (Bonnie) Liang, Yifei Sun, Suyang (Susan) Wang, Yucheng Wang, Will Weinstein, Yodsadhorn (Calvin) Vinitwatanakhun, Steven Yu, Youyuan (Catherine) Zhang.

Thank you to my dear colleagues at the Stevens Institute of Technology: Brian Rothschild, Ph.D., Pete Dominic, Ph.D., Caitlin McClure, Steve Gogel.

Thank you to my past and current A-team colleagues at Baruch College: Debbie Butler, Fred Burke, Annie Himmelsbach, Ellen King, Greg Leporati, Jennifer Seidman, Justyn Makarewycz, Lindsey Plewa, Jack Pullara.

Gratitude to my professional BFFs at the Financial Women's Association: Annette Stewart, Hermina (Nina) Batson, Anastasia Boukouvala, MBA, Cornelia Levy-Bencheton.

About the Author

Nancy Ancowitz is a career strategist. She's also a career director at NYU, and previously, a VP at JPMorgan. She's been speaking, writing about, and coaching introverts since the early 2000s. A pioneer of popular introvert literature, she wrote the book *Self-Promotion for Introverts* (McGraw Hill) and has been published by *The New York Times* and *The Wall Street Journal*; she blogs for *Psychology Today* and *The Times*

of Israel. As a career coach, she helps clients communicate their gifts to the world authentically. They do this by creating a powerful personal brand and sharpening presentation skills, online and in person. This can be life-changing—they get the job, the promotion, or the recognition they're seeking. For more information, go to nancyancowitz.com.

Also by Nancy Ancowitz

Self-Promotion for Introverts®:
The Quiet Guide to Getting Ahead

Self-Promotion for Introverts® (McGraw Hill) is an indispensable guide that helps introverts excel in an extroverts' world. Nancy shows you how to use your introversion to your advantage. Get heard more even if you talk less. Jump-start your visibility and climb to new heights in your career.

Get noticed . . . and get ahead!